Communion Confirmation and Commitment

Some current issues in Christian Initiation

by

C. H. B. Byworth

Lecturer at Oak Hill College, Southgate, London

SBN 910710 51 2

GROVE BOOKS

BRAMCOTE NOTTS.

CONTENTS

PREFATORY NOTE TO SECOND EDITION

The first edition of this booklet was published in 1972, and in it I here expressed my thanks for the help received from the Latimer House Liturgy Group, my colleagues at Oak Hill, and in particular to John Simpson. Now, after the booklet has been out of print for some months, it has been possible to incorporate into a second edition some mention of the Synod debate and resolution of February 1974. This has involved some changes in the Introduction on pages 3–5. But it has seemed best to leave the rest of the booklet to stand unchanged.

Christopher Byworth,

13 June, 1974

First Edition September 1972
Second Edition July 1974

SBN 901710 51 2

1. INTRODUCTION

The scope of this booklet is ambitious. It aims to raise virtually all the crucial and controversial initiation issues, to suggest the outline of a new service and set out a new pastoral policy. The main issues raised include the whole question of the nature of initiation, and in particular another discussion on the nature and meaning of baptism and confirmation. This leads into a discussion of the biblical attitude to children in general, since this way of approaching the initiation issues is often neglected. A new service is sketched out and defended, though it is not, of course, intended for uncritical adoption into use, but it shows the lines along which the theological and pastoral suggestions made here could be implemented liturgically.

The service has been called 'The Service of Commitment and Commissioning'. It will be noted that the term 'Confirmation' has been completely dropped, since the ceremony is unlike what we have traditionally known as 'Confirmation', though the ratification of baptismal vows is included in it[1]. The pastoral suggestions spell out how these new principles could be worked out for different groups of people, and then discuss the various issues involved.

The intention throughout has been to suggest a new and better way ahead since dissatisfaction with several aspects of our present pattern is understandably mounting. An attempt has been made to base all the suggestions on biblical principles and priorities, whilst giving at least some place to the existing breadth of widely varying Anglican theological outlooks on confirmation. The suggestions for a parish policy have again tried to be broad enough to cope with differing approaches to questions like baptismal discipline.

The above paragraphs were written for the first edition of this booklet in the Summer of 1972. At that point the Ely Report *Christian Initiation: Birth and Growth in the Christian Society*[2] had hardly been considered in the Church of England. Now, however, its contents have become the subject of resolutions of General Synod, and these are being referred to the dioceses for wider debate. This necessitates the new edition of the booklet.

The first General Synod resolution concerned policies in respect of infant baptism.[3] The second relates very closely to the present booklet. It was passed at the same session in February 1974, and ran as follows:

> 'That this Synod, recognising that there are divergent theological understandings of Christian Initiation held within the Church:
> (i) accepts the principle that full sacramental participation within the Church may precede a mature Profession of Faith;
> (ii) invites the Standing Committee to ask the dioceses if they

1 Here the Ely Commission are to my mind, changing the role and purpose of the ceremony but hanging onto the name 'Confirmation'.

2 This was originally published by C.I.O. in 1971 for 40p. Now it has been combined with *Baptism, Thanksgiving and Blessing* in a single production (C.I.O. 1974, 60p.)

3 This is set out and discussed in the second edition of Booklet 3 in this series, *Baptismal Discipline* by Colin Buchanan, and does not directly concern us here.

would support a re-ordering of initiation practice according to this principle by one or more of the following means within a continuing framework of training for the Christian life;

(a) admission of baptised persons to the Holy Communion at the discretion of the parish priest in consultation with the Bishop followed by Confirmation at the hands of the Bishop;

(b) uniting the laying on of hands and/or anointing with oil to Baptism followed, after due preparation, by admission to the Holy Communion at the discretion of the parish priest: and subsequently providing an opportunity, where appropriate, for a solemn affirmation of baptismal promises accompanied by a further laying on of hands;

and to report their views to the Secretary-General by January 1976.'

It will be noted that paragraph (i) in this resolution commits the Synod to a similar view to chapter 3 below, whilst paragraph (ii) opens the question discussed in chapter 2 below, and further covered in the Appendixes. It may prove difficult for the dioceses to focus on the question at issue, but it really concerns the sufficiency of water baptism as sacramental initiation. Since, on the showing of this booklet, extra ceremonies are non-provable from the Bible and from the first two centuries of the Christian Church, and since they cannot have the theological significance often attributed to them concerning the Spirit, it seems best to omit them altogether from the initiatory rite, or at most to make them optional. The widespread misunderstanding of the meaning of the giving of the sign of the cross in baptism is a warning to be heeded. If to this we add the current questionable views about the meaning of the laying on of hands, whether the ceremony is joined to baptism or not, we shall have reason enough to reject any insistence upon such a ceremony as a necessary part of Christian initiation.

This means that the dioceses would be well advised to accept (ii)(a) and to reject (ii)(b). If this is done weightily and widely then General Synod could well endorse the findings. If the dioceses prove to have a large minority strongly insisting on (ii)(b) (and actually rejecting (ii)(a)), then, and perhaps only then, ought the olive-branch located in Appendix 1 in this booklet to be seriously considered. The General Synod has accepted a way of handling the question which will give it data upon which to decide the matter.

If paragraph (i) of the General Synod resolution is accepted by the dioceses then it will give opportunity to a reconsideration of the role and proper age for 'Confirmation'. The present role includes the admission to Communion (which would then be detached from it) and the rite comes at an age too young for adult profession of faith. If the rite is *not* about the coming of the Spirit, then its remaining feature, this adult profession of faith or 'Commitment', can come into greater prominence and occur at a more sensible age.

In the changes suggested here I am also attempting to integrate 'Commitment' with assumption of particular responsibilities in a way not mentioned in any official report[1]. A more positive function is here given to the Electoral Roll. The Church of England has been attempting to make these Rolls more realistic in removing 'dead wood' from them, but the need is as much to make them more relevant in setting out and consolidating an actual working membership list for the local church. The Rolls are the only way in which members of the Church of England can in fact 'belong' to a local church. The minimum age for admission to them is 17, at which age the Church of England is presumably ready to treat persons as 'adult'. As that would be exactly the purpose of the 'commitment' rite a very happy coalescing of functions is possible. 'Commitment' would not be just a public declaration, it would also involve the assumption of electoral and governmental responsibilities, and include 'membership'[2] of the local church. Whereas at the moment, therefore, the 'sacramental' and the 'governmental' features of membership are completely divorced from each other, in the new rite they would become one.

In the rite there is also a corporate dedication to Christ of the whole congregation. It is precisely this aspect of baptism, the making of the vows, which is being renewed by the candidates in the proposed annual service of 'commitment'. Thus after each has done this individually for the first time the opportunity comes for the whole congregation to renew these promises corporately in the context of a communion service. Again the Ely report has hinted at this possibility in paragraph 149. It would of course be in some ways similar to, and a point in common with, the Methodist 'Covenant' service.

It is clear that such a 'commitment' service would not absolutely require the bishop's presence—and if it were to occur in each parish annually (instead of once for a whole group of parishes, as is currently the practice with confirmation) then it might be difficult with large present dioceses to make the bishop's presence a rule. But it is important that the bishop's role as president of the eucharist should be strengthened, and it would be highly desirable that he should preside at *this* eucharist almost in preference to any others.

Finally, the suggestions made here ought to be relevant to the ecumenical situation. The Ely Commission in Appendix 2 of their report have set out the areas of agreement already reached, and particularly significant is the growing agreement that baptism is the sole rite of initiation. The other questions beyond that are largely secondary—though the continuing divide (which is *through* as well as *between* denominations) over the propriety of baptising infants at all is a very deep one. Nothing contained here should make ecumenical agreement *harder* to reach.

[1] The Ely Commission may hint at this idea: 'If this rite were to be administered in this way in adult life it would be fittingly related to the assumption of responsibilities in the synodically governed church.' (Paragraph 123).

[2] For 'membership' in its most important aspect, i.e. being in communion, then, it must be emphasised, baptism alone admits to membership. But it is difficult to make this universal qualification also simultaneously involve membership of both the Church of England nationally and a particular local parish. Hence these derivative concepts of 'membership'.

2. BAPTISM AND CONFIRMATION: DOCTRINAL ISSUES

It is clearly beyond the scope of so short a booklet to do much more about doctrinal foundations than to state one's conclusions and one's main reasons for holding them.

Firstly, the only essential 'ingredients' in the New Testament rite of baptism are the application of water and the name of Jesus. Perhaps it is unnecessary to enter again the somewhat foolish discussion over the amount of water and method of applying. More serious worries could arise over the fact that, whereas in Acts baptism is usually 'into the name of Jesus', in Mt. 28.19, in the Didache (perhaps to be dated to 120 AD), and at least arguably in the writings of Justin Martyr (around 160 AD), baptism is into the name of the Trinity. However, this need not delay us since Mt. 28.19 may not actually be a baptismal formula and the change to the Trinitarian name was a natural one as the church became increasingly aware of the doctrinal implications of its own Trinitarian experience of God.

Secondly, it follows negatively that neither the laying on of hands,[1] (with or without prayer for the coming of the Spirit and irrespective of whether or not these hands are episcopal) nor the pouring on or signing with oil can be seen as a regular essential part of the baptismal rite.

On four occasions only in the New Testament (Acts 8.4-24; 19.1-7; 9.17-19; Heb. 6.2-4) is it possible to argue that the laying on of hands was used in initiation i.e. associated with baptism. Each time the Spirit is connected with the ceremony. However in Paul's case, Acts 9.17-19, the reason for the laying on of hands is as much healing as the giving of the Spirit and he is baptized *afterwards.* The other six instances of baptism in Acts (2.41; 8.38; 10.48; 16.15; 33; 18.8) do not mention any laying on of hands. Indeed Acts 2.38 specifically makes the point that the outward sign that gives the Spirit is baptism.[2]

To assert the probability, or even the possibility, that hands were both always laid on in New Testament times and brought the Spirit raises other problems too. How did Cornelius receive the Spirit *without* hands being laid on him (Acts 10.44)? Were they then laid on afterwards? We read of water, but not of this. And why is the laying on of hands not mentioned in the other baptisms in Acts? If it be answered that they were taken for granted, then Philip's omission to lay his hands on the Samaritans, which seems clearly implied in Acts 8.12, is incredible, and it was totally predictable that the Spirit would not come upon them at their baptism! Furthermore, if it needed *apostles'* hands to be imposed, then Philip ought not to have gone off baptising in the wilderness and the Ethiopian eunuch ought not to have gone on his way rejoicing—he had been only half-initiated.

1 The various contents and meanings for 'confirmation' in the Church of England together with the various purposes for which hands were laid on in the Bible are set out in Appendix 2. An alternative position possibly more acceptable to some in the Church of England is set out in Appendix 1.

2 This is not of course to argue that the Spirit can *only* come in baptism. 1 Cor. 1.14 would be an astonishing remark if this were so. Only repentance and faith are needed (Acts 11.17; 19.2; Gal. 3.2), though these were almost invariably expressed in baptism. Neither Apollos nor the apostles seem to have received baptism into the name of Jesus, but both most probably received John's baptism (Acts 18.25; Jn. 1.37; 4.2) and of course knew about Jesus' teaching (Acts 18.25). Both also had received the Spirit, the disciples at Pentecost, Apollos we know not when (Acts 18.25). Thus inward and outward were not always and inevitably tied together.

Nor are the omissions confined to the Acts. The laying on of hands is not mentioned in Mt. 28.19, nor in Paul's many references to baptism. Paul's silence is particularly striking as he frequently writes of Christians having received the Spirit. Dunn is, of course, right that the experience of the Spirit is more important to Paul than any rite with water or the laying on of hands; nevertheless for Paul the Spirit and baptism were closely associated (1 Cor. 12.13 and possibly 6.11) whereas the Spirit and the laying on of hands are only associated in Paul's writings in 2 Tim. 1.6 in a context which looks like ordination rather than initiation. Some have tried to override the contrary evidence of Acts 8.12 by saying that Philip was no apostle, hence the lack of hands. But this proves far too much. Quite apart from the incident of the Ethiopian eunuch already mentioned, it opens up the faintly ridiculous idea of the Jerusalem apostles travelling the ancient world laying hands on those professing faith after their baptism. Thus *prima facie* Acts 8 and 19 are the exceptions[1] and the burden of proof lies strongly on those who want to assert that they are the norm. Acts 8 is hardly a useful text for those who want hands laid on *at the same time as* baptism. What it might support is a second, later initiatory act of the laying on of hands bringing the Spirit, but such an idea is without parallel anywhere in the New Testament (including Acts 19) and contradicts other basic New Testament teaching on the Spirit (see page 11). It is therefore better to see Acts 8 as exceptional and look elsewhere for an explanation (see Appendix 4). Acts 19.5-6 does however seem to describe one rite of initiation with two parts, baptism and the laying on of hands. But Paul's question 'into what then were you baptized?' asked just after they have said that they have never even heard that there was a Holy Spirit, shows that for Paul the Spirit is linked to baptism not to the laying on of hands. The laying on of hands here (as in Acts 8) may be to merge those of some Christian standing into mainstream Christianity (see Appendix 3). Heb. 6.2-4 next demands our attention. Among six 'elementary doctrines' laid as a foundation for these very probably Jewish Christians, now in danger of apostasy (in Rome?), are mentioned together 'teaching of baptisms [Greek *"baptismon"*] and [Greek: *"te"*] the laying on of hands.' Verse 4 goes on to talk of those 'who have once been enlightened, who have tasted the heavenly gift and have become partakers of the Holy Spirit.' The aorist tenses in verse 4 ,the term 'enlightened' which Justin was to use in Rome in 160 AD to describe baptism and which may be hinted at in the New Testament, all suggest a reference to baptism, and so on the surface does the word *'baptismon'* in verse 2. In this case, there is here a reference to a ceremony of initiation including baptism and the laying on of hands and associated with the coming of the Holy Spirit. It is one ceremony with two parts, baptism with water and the laying on of hands (the word *'te'* for 'and' implies a closer linking than the normal Greek word for 'and' would do). This fits with Acts 19, but not with the time-lag of Acts 8. The main problem of the Hebrews passage is the term *'baptismon'*. Does it or does it not refer to Christian baptism? Bruce (*Hebrews* pp. 114-116) thinks it does not (and the RSV and NEB agree), but rather means 'ablutions'. His

[1] The disciples at Pentecost are *not* parallel since they had only at most received John's baptism and not until Pentecost had the new age of the Spirit dawned fully for any but Jesus, who anticipated this age at his baptism as indeed throughout his life, death and resurrection.

main reason is the fact of the word being in the plural, a form which is never elsewhere used of baptism. The word too is the plural of *'baptismos'* only once used elsewhere of baptism (Col. 2.12 and the text is dubious even here). The usual Greek term is *'baptisma'*. Dunn *(Baptism in the Holy Spirit* pp. 206-7) thinks there must be in context *some* reference to Christian baptism. Maybe the teaching was about the Jewish ablutions and lustrations, of which we see so many at Qumran, and from there the evangelist opened up the subject of Christian baptism. The passage remains a very small and somewhat uncertain piece of evidence on which to found a doctrine over against almost all the rest of the New Testament.

This is the limit of the New Testament evidence for the laying on of hands at initiation; but what about the use of oil, or 'chrism' as this is called? J. D. C. Fisher points out that it was customary among Jews and Greeks to anoint oneself after having a bath, and that 1 Sam. 16.13 links pouring on oil with the coming of the Spirit, though this is far nearer ordination than initiation. M. Moreton (*Theology,* Nov. 1971) argues for Christian initiation rites being partly based on or assimilated to Gentile and Jewish purificatory rites and asks pertinently where and when such chrisms arose, since they are clearly part of the initiatory rite by Tertullian's and Hippolytus' time. However, granting all this, the case for even *a* practice of anointing, let alone *the regular* practice, at initiation in the New Testament period is extremely thin. The word group occurs infrequently and only in 2 Cor. 1.21; 1 Jn. 2.20, 27 could it refer to an initiation rite. The verses mentioning sealing, i.e. Eph. 1.13; 4.30, have sometimes been adduced as further evidence, and 2 Cor. 1.21 includes both terms; but Lampe has shown that both the latter and the former types of terminology are far more likely to refer to baptism. Other uses of the word-group are clearly figurative. Lk. 4.18 quoting Is. 61.1, Heb. 1.9 and Acts 10.38 and possibly 4.27 refer to what God did to Jesus at His baptism. 1 Jn. 2.20, 27 can hardly be literal since the chrism not only abides in them, but also teaches them (compare Jn. 14.26 where this is the Spirit's function). If it did refer to oil given at initiation then presumably the 'heretics' who 'went out from us' would have received it as well; and John could scarcely argue that it would protect the genuine Christians from the others. 2 Cor. 1.21 can hardly refer to an anointing either. Dunn, contra Lampe, doubts whether it even refers to baptism (Lampe may well be supported by the remark in *The Shepherd* of Hermas 'the seal is the water') and thinks the gift of the Spirit is referred to. The only literal use of oil recorded seems to be for healing, Jas. 5.14.

It is essential to look next at the later evidence down to 250 AD to see whether and how soon either the laying on of hands or the use of oil or prayer for the Holy Spirit are found.[1] The laying on of hands and the use of oil are found in Tertullian and Hippolytus, but not clearly found any earlier i.e. than about 200-220 AD. The remarks of Justin, especially in his *Dialogue,* have been interpreted by E. C. Ratcliffe in *Theology* 1948 to refer to laying on of hands, and M. Moreton *(Theology* Nov. 1971 and June 1972) tries to sustain this, but certainly A. T. Hanson (*Theology* April 1972) is correct in saying that no rite is actually mentioned nor *prima facie* implied.

[1] The important and fascinating later history of 'confirmation' is briefly and not tendentiously sketched in paragraphs 85 to 88 of the Ely report and traces the break up of the developed third century rite of baptism-'confirmation'-first communion in the Western church and the new meanings sought for and given to Confirmation.

However, Theophilus of Antioch's remark around AD 180 'we therefore are called Christians for this reason that we are anointed with the oil of God' could well be taken literally of chrism, presumably at initiation. This is not however a vast amount of evidence, and it is hard to resist A. T. Hanson's conclusion: 'the evidence that any such rite existed during the first two centuries is minimal and certainly not such as to oblige the church to regard a complementary rite of initiation as essential'. The use of oil and the laying on of hands were certainly present by 200 AD in parts of the church at least and were universal later in the third century. The reasons for this may well have been similarity to Gentile and other Jewish customs, and the laying on of hands could be argued from Acts 8 and 19. However, in the light of the known tendency of other ceremonies to creep in, it seems speculative to insist that these particular two arose from the New Testament period. Therefore the only definite evidence in the New Testament and for a century afterwards is for a rite using water in the name of Jesus or of the Trinity, a rite called baptism that only on exceptional occasions included the laying on of hands or other ceremony. Beyond that we cannot go.

The third and final conclusion complements this. It is that baptism signifies and is intimately associated with *all* that God does in Christ for the believer, especially the crucial and distinctive giving of the Spirit, and that therefore there is no aspect of initiation outstanding that the laying on of hands or any other subsequent act could signify, and especially not the giving of the Spirit. Let us see first what general truths are signified by baptism.

In the Bible baptism and God's word proclaimed and received with faith are both said to have the effects of regeneration (Jn. 3.5 compare Jas. 1.18 and 1 Pet. 1.23), the forgiveness of sins (Acts 2.38; 22.16 compare Acts 13.38,39), and making men sons of God (Gal. 3.27 compare Gal. 3.26).[1] Indeed in Acts 19.4,5 and Gal. 3.26,27 the terms 'be baptized' and 'believe—have faith' seem virtually interchangeable. Baptism is also said to unite a man with Christ in his death and burial (Rom. 6.1-10; Col. 2.12) and to incorporate him into Christ's body, the Church (1 Cor. 12.10-13 possibly also Eph. 4.4). As was stated above, none of this evidence means that baptism automatically conveyed these effects. Such teaching as Rom. 2.25-29 on circumcision would surely imply this by parallel, as would Peter's remarks in verses 21 to 24 in the Acts 8 incident, Paul's disclaimer in 1 Cor. 1.14 and indeed the whole emphasis on the need to respond. Dunn is right to stress this point. But on the other hand, as against Dunn, the outward and inward are very closely linked[2] so that in a real sense it seems possible to say that in some ways neither is complete apart from the other. Surely the explanation lies partly in the fact that, in the New Testament church, the context was always one of missionary preaching where response was followed by immediate baptism. There is no case recorded in Acts of a delayed baptism; and Paul seems to assume that all in the churches of Rome and Colossae (and presumably elsewhere) have been baptized. Thus it made sense to look back either to one's baptism or to one's conversion equally, when claiming their effects for one's Christian

[1] I am indebted for this particular presentation of the evidence to an article by R. T. Beckwith ('The Age of Admission to Communion', *The Churchman,* Spring, 1971).

[2] This link is well stated by C. O. Buchanan in *Evangelical Essays on Church and Sacraments* (SPCK, 1972), pp.52-54.

life now. It could well be argued that today in Britain, with dropping numbers of those applying for baptism and of definite converts to Christianity, the time is ripe to reintroduce immediate adult (and family!) baptism on profession. At any rate Paul presumed that all those who had been baptized were believers and treated them thus, though this did not prevent him or other New Testament writers (see especially Heb. 6.1-8; 10.26-31) from dire warnings when things were going seriously wrong in a church.[1]

However, one of the key issues for this booklet is whether the coming of the Spirit is primarily associated with baptism or with the laying on of hands. J. D. C. Fisher in *Confirmation and the Ely Report* writes 'The Report [i.e. Ely] claims that the gift of the Spirit was received in a simple rite of baptism in water without any further ceremonies. Yet the number of occasions when St. Paul associates the gift of the Spirit with baptism in water are comparatively few, there are fourteen places where he refers to the reception of the Spirit without mentioning baptism or any other sacramental act at all.' (p.4). The latter point is simply met by asserting with Dunn that the inward Spirit-experience was more important for Paul than the outward act, however vital the latter. But even the former point does not prove what Fisher wants, for Paul certainly nowhere associates an initiatory coming of the Spirit with the laying on of hands.

Positively, however, the Holy Spirit is associated with baptism often and overwhelmingly in the New Testament. This does not depend on whether or not we see, with Lampe, a reference to baptism in the 'seal-anointing' verses (2 Cor. 1.21; Eph. 1.13; 4.30 1 Jn. 2.20,27). I still do—despite Dunn's pleas, which arise, I suspect, from his right emphasis on the experience of the Spirit rather than the outward act of water baptism. But to stress the former does not exclude the latter, particularly when the aorist tenses are used, the Pauline verses are linked to Christ (compare Rom. 6.1-10) and *The Shepherd* of Hermas soon after the New Testament period can state dogmatically 'the seal then is the water'. The picture of

1 The significance of baptism is so well summed up in two paragraphs of the Ely Commission's report that it seems worthwhile quoting them both:

'The background of this history is the practice and theology of Baptism interpreted in various ways by the different New Testament writers. About its practice in the primitive Church we know little. Its theology, however, reaches its fullest and richest expression in St. Paul. For him Baptism is the sacrament of all that is meant by "in Christ". It is the visible sign and efficacious symbol of God's gracious approach to man in Christ and man's response of faith. It applies to the believer the full totality of the gospel. This can be apprehended under many aspects: washing from sin, justification, sanctification, salvation, and so on; but all these are subsumed under the central conviction that believers are united, by the action of God, with Christ in His death and resurrection. They are made sons of God in Christ; and this is another way of saying that they are indwelt by the Spirit of God (cf. Rom. 8.15; Gal. 4.6). Union with Christ, effected through grace which evokes faith, and sacramentally shown forth in Baptism, implies incorporation into the Church, the body of Christ and the spirit-possessed community which is the sphere of the koinonia of the Holy Spirit.' [Paragraph 76].

'Baptism signifies: (a) the totality of God's creative and redemptive work for us and (b) the totality of the father/son relationship in Christ/Holy Spirit realised through grace/faith, which God has thereby established. Therefore Baptism cannot be added to, supplemented, or "completed". It is the one and complete sacrament of Christian initiation, and the whole course of Christian life up to and beyond death should be a progressive realisation of what Baptism effectively declares in a single sacramental moment' [Paragraph 69].

sealing as stamping a person or thing as one's own also fits baptism, where we are stamped as Christ's by going through his experience and anointing ('Christ' means Messiah, the anointed one) at his baptism in Jordan.

However the link between baptism and the Holy Spirit is secure and basic on other grounds:- Firstly, it is made explicit as the unique new feature about the baptism which Jesus both received and was to give to others through his disciples. This occurred from Pentecost onwards, as they followed him in entering into the benefits of the new age of fulfilment (Mk. 1.8; Jn. 1.33; Acts 2.17). Secondly, the link between the risen Jesus and the Spirit is basic in all strata of the New Testament; in Luke as the gift of the ascended Christ which he received from the Father (Acts 2.33; 5.32); in John as from the Father through the Son (Jn. 15.26), bringing Jesus to the disciples (Jn. 16.15) and binding them to him (1 Jn. 3.24; 4:13); and perhaps supremely in Paul for whom the Spirit is the Spirit of Christ (Gal. 4.6; Phil. 1.19). In Rom. 8.9-10. Paul talks in immediate succession of the Spirit of God in them, as them having Christ's Spirit and as Christ being in them. No wonder Lampe, (*Seal of the Spirit,* p.50) talks of Paul's 'synthesis between the traditional idea of the Spirit and his own Christ-mysticism', though Dunn (in *Journal of Theological Studies* Oct. 1970) has shown that Lampe was probably wrong to add that Paul identifies Son and Spirit in 2 Cor. 3.17. Thirdly, baptism was supremely into the name of Jesus and thus was into or in or by the Spirit. In particular the baptized were now experiencing the Holy Spirit as Christ had at his baptism. He was the same Holy Spirit (Acts 10.38, 44), and so as Lampe says 'by participation in the Anointed they receive a share of His anointing' (p.52). In Paul, because of his Christ-mysticism, this idea is most clearly expressed, as in 1 Cor. 12:13 'for by one Spirit we were all baptized into one body . . . and all were made to drink of the one Spirit'. There is no way of dividing Rom. 6.1-10 with its baptism into Christ from Rom. 8.1-17 on the Spirit, and especially Rom. 8.9 'anyone who does not have the Spirit of Christ does not belong to him'. Thus not only does baptism signify all that the Christian life has to offer, but in particular since it is baptism into Christ, it is very closely linked with reception of the Spirit, reflecting Christ's own baptism.

Should there then be a second later service with the laying on of hands as intended to be initiatory? Or should such a laying on of hands be in the one and only initiatory service? Or should this not occur in initiation at all? The concept of a second initiatory service is conclusively excluded on the New Testament evidence since only Acts 8 could support it. A single, but complex rite has Acts 19 and possibly the more general Heb. 6.2 to support it, but again the whole weight of the New Testament elsewhere seems to be against it. It is hard to see what significance could be given to the other ceremonies in the rite after the administration of the water. The Ely Commission's solution is to encourage the laying on of hands, baptismal anointing and the giving of a lighted candle where they may be desired (paragraph 93), but not to make them obligatory. They remain peripheral.

This leaves us with the norm for Christian sacramental initiation as solely baptism in water in the name of the Trinity, as this alone can be proved from the New Testament, and it is to baptism alone that all initiatory significance, and in particular the gift of the Spirit, attaches. A corollary arising from this is that there is no warrant from the New Testament nor from early church history for insisting upon any further rite than baptism as a condition for entry into the holy communion. To this now we must turn.

3. CHILDREN AT COMMUNION— SOME BIBLICAL FACTORS

Perhaps one of the most serious omissions of the Ely report is its failure even to mention the doctrinal issues raised by its suggestion to allow baptized children to take the Lord's Supper after instruction, at perhaps the age of nine, but before confirmation. Psychological and educational factors are scarcely mentioned either in this regard, though there is a nod to Piaget. It is quite beyond any experience or ability of mine to tackle this latter aspect, though there are experts in the educational field who would defend what is proposed here. Rather the present chapter constitutes an attempt to formulate the barest outline of a biblical doctrine of children in so far as it has bearing on the age of admission to communion.[1] I believe the issue is dealt with more profoundly when the whole question of the status of the child from a home of professing believers is examined.

The Old Testament and Judaism will be examined first, and three aspects are particularly scrutinised. Firstly, it seems clear that the child is seen as part of a family unit rather than as an individual, and thus is treated as having the same status as a believer as his parents and particularly his father. The child belongs in a profound way to his family, and to his father, who can even be described as his ba'al or owner. Thus his importance is that he is a gift from God (Gen. 30.2), perpetuating the Father's name (Deut. 25.5,6) (hence the special desire for sons) and being the future Israel in the making, and the correct parent-child relationship is a condition of the covenant itself (Ex. 20.12). This oneness with the family is the reason why the covenant sign is given (Gen. 17.1). Secondly, there does seem to be the concept that the child has at least some spiritual awareness of its own. Of this the classic example is Samuel who grows in his understanding of the Lord (1 Sam. 2.21,26; 3.19), and is personally addressed by Yahweh. The child's main responsibility is to learn, as the Father's is to teach, (Deut. 6.6, 20). He does of course 'come of age' at various times for various functions, but the idea of a spiritual relationship to God, at first perhaps in and through his parents, does seem to be taught.

The third question is how far the child took part in worship and in particular in the Passover. This almost certainly varied at differing times in Jewish history; but undoubtedly the child took part in the religious training that took place in the home, and that included circumcision and, for many folk for most of Israel's history, the Passover. No doubt children stayed in the court of women in the Temple, but could still take in the worship to some extent from there. As for the synagogue, the children would presumably have again participated as much as the women. R. T. Beckwith has set out,[2] perhaps over-exactly, the varying estimates within the Old Testament and Judaism of the correct age for particular functions. In the light of Jeremias'

[1] I am indebted to an unpublished paper by the Rev. J. Pridmore for some of the points made here.

[2] The article quoted on page 9 above, from which all further quotations by Beckwith are cited.

researches (*Eucharistic Words of Jesus* S.C.M. pp.15-88) into the Lord's Supper, it is more than likely that this meal was either a passover meal or an anticipated passover meal a day early, and Beckwith argues that in Jesus' time it was not necessarily a family meal since only the men over 20 go up to Jerusalem, (Deut. 16.5-7,16; Ex. 23.17; 34.23). The evidence seems inconclusive. On the one hand the 12 seem to have been alone and the above-quoted verses could be taken exclusively of men only, though a knowledgeable rabbi, with whom I have spoken, thought this improbable. On the other hand the Mishnah clearly foresees women, slaves and minors partaking (Pesahim 8.1,5,7). The son is to ask the father 'Why is this night different from other nights?' and the Mishnah adds 'if the son has not enough understanding, his father instructs him' (Pesahim 10.4). The tradition was also that it should be the youngest son. Beckwith quotes the Mishnah (Pesahim 8.7) that the minimum amount of meat to be eaten to qualify for membership of the Passover company is an olive's bulk. This might well exclude actual infants, though hardly very young children, and 'minors' are mentioned as present in the same section. Josephus (*Antiquities* 11:4:8, 109f) clearly believed that before AD 70 the women and children did go up to the feast. Jeremias (*Eucharistic Words* pp.50,85) reckons that the child's question was part of the Passover ritual in Jesus' time which might well suggest that children were still present frequently. We see the boy Jesus, aged 12, coming up for the pilgrim feast in Lk. 2.41-43.

What conclusions can be reached? On the Passover, what started as a family meal where the children were present[1] (Ex. 12.26f), became, probably at the time of Josiah's reforms, a pilgrim feast. Josephus' evidence suggests that women and children did go to this before AD 70. The evidence of the Mishnah is notoriously hard to date. Some passages clearly envisage children taking part, if not infants, and seem to refer to the time before the fall of Jerusalem. Children have certainly been included since. The balance of probability, taken with the principle of children joining in with their parents wherever possible as part of the family unit, suggests that only practical considerations would have prevented children taking part in the Passover meal. In the New Testament period, where the Lord's Supper was part of a family meal to start with and held in the home, it is hard to see both why and how the children could have been excluded, at least among Jewish Christians.

Jesus' attitude to children was to give them a radically new importance. Jeremias (*New Testament Theology* Vol. I p.227) claims that such sayings as Mk. 10.14; Mt. 18.3 mean that Jesus 'brings children nearer to God than adults'. This would be on the grounds of their objective need, and the fact that they were then generally despised. This of course fits Jesus' special and messianic concern for the 'poor' (Mt. 11.5). However, probably no conclusions can be drawn from this about whether they should be present at communion. More helpful may be the rest of the New Testament's tendency, continued from the Old Testament and Judaism, to treat children as part of the family unit (Col. 3.21; Eph. 6.1-4; Heb. 12.5-11; 1 Tim. 3.4,12). J. A. Simpson, in an unpublished paper, has pointed out

[1] And if present would they not have taken part in the meal as well as asking the question, especially as the ground for eating the passover was circumcision (Ex. 12.43-49)?

that disobedience to parents is included in 'unchristian' behaviour and this again implies that the children are being treated and thought of as Christians, presumably growing in their response to God as they grow in age like Samuel, and even in a sense like the child Jesus, (Lk. 2.52). Up until the end of the third century, with the possible exception of Aristides and Hermas, the same attitude continues.

Such an attitude, expressed naturally by the baptism in infancy of the children of believing parents, seems to me to lead to the suggestion that they be treated as Christians in every way possible, including participation in the Christian family meal from the earliest possible age. The Ely report (para. 134) hints that children should not be admitted till 9 years old. The problem of fixing an age, besides that of theological inconsistency, is to decide what age. A child can express a definite faith at 5 years old or younger. The possibility of bringing, say, three children to the rail and only allowing the oldest to receive, seems hard to justify on grounds of theology.

Objections to this suggestion will arise. Firstly, how does this relate to the place of understanding, faith and repentance as a prior necessity? Beckwith rightly rejects the objection that it is essential to be able to remember Christ's death and examine oneself as in 1 Cor. 11.23-32, since this proves too much (on such grounds, infants should not be baptized either). But Beckwith does argue against infant, and less strongly against child, communion on the grounds of what he calls the prerequisite of baptism. By this he seems to mean that the baptism of infants is 'incomplete' until they have personally professed faith and repentance; and since baptism is the formal gateway to communion, baptized infants should be barred from entry until their baptism is 'completed' by such a personal profession. Accepting this argument for a moment, it is clear that it would not preclude from communion quite young children from Christian homes where, by the age of five if not before, they may well be expressing in their own, albeit theologically inadequate, way their love for the Lord Jesus, and could no doubt express it formally if so required. However there seems to be confusion over the difference between the efficacy and completeness of baptism. An infant's baptism is undoubtedly *complete* liturgically when repentance and faith have been expressed in response to God's word, and water has been administered in the name of the Trinity. When it becomes *efficacious* lies in God's hands, since covenant theology suggests that we are to presume that the child is in the covenant from the start and treat him accordingly. Thus the demand to await 'efficacy' is an impractical one, as it would indeed be also for an adult whose profession of faith and repentance might be false, even though the church must treat it as true. The church must treat the baptized (even young children) *as believers,* rather than as merely potential believers. If it cannot do this, it should not baptize them. If it can do this, it should admit the baptized to communion.

Beckwith's second objection is part of his argument that the parallel between infant baptism and infant communion is not sufficient to establish the latter. It will have been noticed that my own reasons are more widely based and include the whole status of children in the bible. However Beckwith's objection here is that milk, not solid food such as bread, let alone wine, is the suitable food for an infant. Thus while it is suitable to give an infant a (symbolic) wash, bread and wine are not suitable food and drink. However the whole objection seems irrelevant, as the congruity of the element is simply not part of the argument in respect of either sacrament.

Beckwith's other objection is that infant communion, as a practice, is not attested so early as is infant baptism in the first centuries of the church. He disallows the implication in Hippolytus, on the grounds that, though the infants were baptized, they are not specified in the ensuing communion. However the opening rubric (21.4-5) which specifies the baptizing of infants and women seems to cover the whole initiation rite including communion. If it be argued that since the children are not specifically mentioned at communion they were withdrawn, it would be proper to reply that this lack of mention would include the women also, who must on this supposition also have been withdrawn. Anyway there is evidence by Cyprian's time (250 AD) of the practice, though Origen may show that it was an issue in dispute. As the earliest definite evidence of infant baptism is about 200 AD, this is hardly a major difference.

A fourth objection is that a young child may not be able to respond and learn. This has just been dealt with. However, once infancy is past such an objection is a matter for the education experts. The audio-visual drama of the eucharist properly performed, is arguably an *easier* way for a quite young child to take in at least something of the great truths enshrined in this service than is much verbalising; and it is of course assumed that suitable instruction will be being given each Sunday as well, preferably separately in the 'Bible' half of the service.

A more serious objection is that to open the sacraments to all would encourage a purely formal Christianity. This may well be true. But the proposal here is not one of opening the sacraments to all without distinction. What is being recommended is communion for the baptized children of at least one communicant parent, when that parent attends communion along with his child.

Finally it has been suggested that to give communion so young to children is to leave them nothing to look forward to in adulthood, and to 'spoil' them young, following the trend of our age today. However, this argument seems to prove too much. For if we are to keep the best till later, why do we encourage children to participate in prayer and bible reading, the other means of grace (and the latter is a considerably more intellectualised exercise) ? If the Lord's Supper is truly a means of meeting with and feeding on Christ, then surely we should encourage our children to appreciate and use it as such ? If they have need of God's grace at all, how can we deny them this means of grace ?

4. LITURGICAL ISSUES

Once the respective roles and ages for baptism and admission to communion have been demarcated, there arises the question of the 'coming of age' enrolment service. It will not include the 'coming of the Holy Spirit'. It will not include admission to holy communion. It will not be initiatory. What then will it be?

Firstly, its title should be not 'confirmation' but 'commitment'. 'Confirmation' includes too many overtones of the present anomalous practice and competing theologies.

Secondly, such a service should be held annually, preferably within a communion service, and should include a rededication by renewal of baptismal vows and recommissioning for the whole congregation.

Thirdly, the Bishop should be encouraged to come and preside at the eucharist, but should he lay his hands on the candidates? The service must not look as though it were based on the Samaritan episode in Acts 8, but if neither the presence of the Bishop nor the imposition of his hands were absolutely requisite, then no incorrect doctrinal conclusions could arise. And the laying on of hands has a certain appropriateness. Acts 13.1-3, and 2 Tim. 1.6, and perhaps Acts 9.17 might be quoted in support of a similar use of laying on of hands for commissioning. If this service were also used, as I believe it should be, for reception of those from other churches into the Church of England, then the laying on of hands might at first be thought desirable along the lines of Dunn's interpretation of Acts 8 and the most likely interpretation of Acts 19. However, this would be inappropriate, for hands were used in these two places for welcoming those who were in no sense really Christians before (hence the coming of the Holy Spirit), and this could hardly be done therefore to Roman Catholics, or Methodists or others (except perhaps Jehovah Witnesses and their like!). Perhaps the best solution is to allow hands to be laid on as an option.

A fourth issue is the repetition of baptismal vows by the individuals in turn, and then by the congregation. The former seems desirable pastorally for the candidate and the church. In one sense it is also desirable theologically for adults to make a second formal statement now (the first was made for them at infant baptism) about their repentance and faith. The latter turns the service into something resembling the Methodist Covenant service, which has some biblical precedent in Deut. 29-31, and Jos. 24, and may well be highly desirable pastorally.

Fifthly, and for this suggestion I am indebted to the Revd. S. Symons, it would seem pastorally wise to tie this service to admission onto the Electoral Roll of the local church. This ,with the renewal of the Roll, has become something of significance at last, and such a link would further heighten its importance. It would also point to 17 as the appropriate age, though some may feel it wiser pastorally to wait till 18, the age of legal majority.

What then would such a service look like? After the introduction to the Communion service in which should be incorporated the penitential material (it would hardly be suitable to have it immediately after the Commissioning!), the readings and sermon should be chosen on the theme of commitment, i.e., God's promises and power to help and our response of dedication, then each individual would personally renew his baptismal vows answering the minister's or bishop's questions. After that the bishop would first welcome him onto the 'membership' roll, and then commission him (perhaps with the laying on of hands). An appropriate formula might be: 'we welcome you . . . now serve Christ . . .' Then the congregation would corporately renew their vows and be re-commissioned. This would lead into what should be a very meaningful Peace and the Communion proper.

The consequential liturgical changes in baptism would be few. Rubrically the laying on of hands would be allowed, though without words, presumably at paragraph 17 of the adult and paragraph 49 of the infant service. It would be left unexplained. If this were thought misleading the Spirit could be further associated with baptism in the blessing of the water. The communicant life could be more strongly in view and 'confirmation' for adults and infants would of course disappear.[1]

[1] It is not part of my aim here, but it is very arguable that a new Series 3 service of baptism with richer language and a different shape would be an improvement on our present, albeit acceptable, Series 2 service.

5. PASTORAL ISSUES

How would it all work out in a parish? This is rightly the first question that any incumbent or laymen, made sceptical by constant appeals to change, always asks. An attempt must now be made to answer this question. Seven different situations can be envisaged.

1. The parents are baptized and communicant and their children are baptized as infants. This may be described as the basic situation. The child may perhaps have been through first a Service of Thanksgiving and Blessing[1], and then has been baptized. When his parents so desire, they quietly bring him to the Lord's table as soon as they think practical. When the child is older, he may well have been in a Sunday School class, and while his friends, whose parents are not in church, go home or are collected from the church hall, he will join his parents in church for the sacramental section of the service. Then assuming his commitment matures in his teens, at the first Commitment and Commissioning Service after he is 17 he is welcomed onto the Electoral Roll, recommits himself personally in the words of the baptism vows, and is commissioned for full adult service in the church. All this would probably be done with the bishop officiating and should lead straight into the eucharist.
2. The parents, whether baptized or not, are non-communicants (or at best three-times-a-year communicants), but the child is baptized and regularly *sent* to Sunday School or sings in the choir. Here is the hardest category to deal with pastorally. The child will have been through baptism, and therefore is formally a Christian and should be allowed to the Lord's table on the covenant principle, but this latter is wearing very thin due to the parents' lack of attendance. Had a stricter baptismal policy been in force, this category would be less large. In principle the child cannot be refused. The actual situation will decide whether he communicates. If he sings in the choir and other children are taking the bread and wine and a more 'general' baptism policy is used, there is little reason to deny him. If a stricter policy is enforced, it would be quite natural to say that communion could be only taken when one of the parents was present, and the choirboy could be allowed to go home rather than stay through the communion or could merely come to the rail for blessing if going home was felt to cause too invidious a distinction.
3. The parents are non-communicant and the child unbaptized but going to Sunday School or Parish Communion. Here one either waits first till the child is 17 and second until there is profession of faith or merely until there is a profession of faith suitable to the child's age, and then one seeks the parents' permission to baptize and admit to communion. This is the 'converted bible-class child' category. Both policies have points in their favour. The former may well prove preferable to those with stricter policies, the latter to those with more open policies.

[1] See Grove Booklet 5 by this name.

4. Churchgoing crypto-Baptist parents with unbaptized children may be a problem, though almost certainly they would not and should not want them to take communion until they profess and are baptized.

5. The unbaptized adult who professes conversion is simply baptized and receives communion as soon as possible. The Commitment and Commissioning service is scarcely necessary as adult baptism has expressed all this already. He would simply take his part in the full life of the Church.

6. Perhaps the greatest 'problem' is the 17 year old, baptized and who has been a communicant but has recently fallen away and now refuses, understandably, to take part in a Commitment and Commissioning service, while, less understandably, continues coming at the three major festivals, to communion. He can hardly be barred as he still professes and he has been fully initiated. However, his lack of commitment is seen in his reluctance to go through this service or come more frequently. Perhaps a quiet word of advice by the minister urging him either to be more committed or to attend non-sacramental services, is all that can be attempted.

7. Reception of an adult, and his family, from another denomination. They will presumably be baptized and thus must be treated as professing and initiated. Since they are already allowed to Anglican communion tables, they can hardly be barred when they join the Church of England. For them a laying on of hands could be used at the Commitment service. This would be their official reception into the Church of England, though on the grounds of their baptism they should be able to receive communion as guests before.

The next practical question is how we move from our present policy to the one outlined above. It should not be too difficult. Once the new slightly different baptism or initiation service were legal and in use, all candidates for baptism, adult or infant, would use it and come into the new structure from then on. Baptized adults and the children of communicant parents would be invited to take the bread and wine (instead of being merely blessed at the rail). Confirmation services would cease and be replaced by the new Commitment and Commissioning Service annually in the local church, preferably with the Bishop present. Those under 17 who are not baptized but profess faith could be encouraged to seek parental permission and be baptized and come to communion. As with baptism policies it might well be right to start such a policy at a diocesan level and hope eventually to win over the General Synod for a national policy.

Finally three general issues not yet discussed need airing briefly. Firstly, what of the Ely Commission's recommendations on children at communion, that preparation was essential and that first communion is of great importance and an occasion for the bishop to be present, if possible? The desire for preparation seems to rest on a false emphasis on the need for understanding. Their right to entry rather rests, primarily on their presumed position in the covenant, and understanding, desirable though it obviously is, will be gained at Sunday School and should be assessed by the individual parents to whom is left the moment to bring their child. Compulsory courses of instruction emphasize too much the first communion, instead of it being simply for the child as natural as coming into one's first big family meal. First communions would also tend to treat children as all equally ready, a point with which parents may not agree; and a parent wanting to delay his child may be pressurized by other church parents when the big event is drawing near. Surely the dangers of first communions being largely social events with white dresses etc., is a thing to be avoided?

Secondly, the difficult problem is raised of what is adult Christian responsibility. Why should the minister speak to the young man in situation six above? Why is the Commitment service needed if the person is already baptized and a communicant? The answer is that although such a person is sacramentally and liturgically initiated and 'adult'; he is not living out the commitment and service implied by these sacraments. Such an outworking would have to include all the main New Testament principles of Christian living, including the full use of one's time and talents, the need for fellowship, service, evangelism, etc. Such can hardly be demonstrated by thrice yearly communion. Thus in coming the man is taking too lightly the commitment implied, and he should be advised of what he is doing and invited to think through what adult commitment means in a course leading to a Commitment service.

Thirdly, how does the new pattern see the bishop's role, which has traditionally been central through confirmation? The Ely Commission has come under attack for the new role given to the bishops, yet in their questionnaire the bishops themselves did not seem to object strongly to a new role, (surely they saw this was implied in the first question asked of them?) It can be argued that the bishop's role is just as much to preside at the eucharist as it is to give confirmation, and the pastoral link with the parishes and adults who are being commissioned will be just as strong, if not stronger, under the new pattern. Another eminently suitable role for the bishop would be taking adult baptisms and presiding at the baptismal eucharist.

Here then is a radical new pattern which, it is hoped, will stimulate discussion, and bible study, and prove acceptable to many differing viewpoints within the church of England. We must do something on this whole complex of initiation issues. My hope is that this slight booklet will stir up thought and action.

APPENDIX 1: THE LAYING ON OF HANDS AS PART OF INITIATION

My own views are clearly set out in chapter 2 above. The laying on of hands should at most be an optional extra in the initiation service. However, I have some sympathy with the pleas of J. D. C. Fisher (*Confirmation and the Ely report* Church Literature Association) and M. Moreton (*Theology* November 1971 and June 1972) that this conclusion put forward in the Ely report would exclude a school of thought in Anglicanism that has a long distinguished pedigree. One could reply that to encourage this where desired is hardly to exclude it, but no doubt Fisher would reply that for 400 years and more the laying on of hands in Confirmation has been compulsory in Anglican churches and that many Anglicans have seen Confirmation as initiatory. He would add that the practice might possibly, to say the least, have New Testament and early church warrant. It is hard to deny this. Reluctantly therefore some such concession as the following is put forward for consideration.

A new initiation service will have to be drafted. It would have to include the use of water and the Trinitarian name as basic, but a laying on of hands is to be admitted. How then will the centrality of water and the Trinitarian name be safeguarded and other ceremonies be seen as subsidiary and explicatory rather than fundamental? Outside the service two ways (see below) will have to suffice. Inside the service, the prayer for the blessing of the water could perhaps specifically request the coming of the Spirit and the baptismal formula could be extended to something like 'I baptize you in the name of the Father who made the world, and in the name of the Son who redeemed mankind, and in the name of the Holy Spirit who indwells and sanctifies the people of God' or if a triple pouring is used, the 'I baptize you' could be thrice repeated (for this suggestion I am grateful to the Rev. J. A. Simpson). The minister's hands are then stretched out over all the candidates and a prayer of the following sort said: 'Almighty, everliving God who has caused these your servants to be born again of water and the Spirit, grant them the Spirit of wisdom and understanding; the Spirit of counsel and inward strength, the Spirit of knowledge and true godliness, and fill them with the Spirit of your holy fear. Amen'. After this the minister would lay hands on each and could anoint each with oil, using the words 'Lord, confirm your servant with your Holy Spirit. Amen'. Then follows immediately the welcome into the fellowship, using something like the statement in Series 2, paragraph 21. The signing with the Cross could come immediately after or, if practical, be restored to its primitive place at the start of the rite. The giving of a lighted candle would be optional and after the cross. The important thing is to retain as one unit of central importance the baptism, laying on of hands and the welcome into the fellowship.

This service would be called baptism, though it could be subtitled 'The Christian service of Initiation'. It would be basically the same for children and adults and should ideally be held within a service of Holy Communion. The title 'Confirmation' has caused such confusion that it would best be dropped, especially as some may want, albeit mistakenly, to interpret the

Commissioning Service thus. Maybe the opportunity could be taken to re-write the whole Series 2 service in the richer and more modern language of Series 3 Holy Communion. Outside the service the fact that the laying on of hands is not essential could be shown in two ways—firstly, in the reception of baptized adults and their families from another denomination into the Church of England. Such should be allowed into communion regularly, as they are now on occasions, after or without some simple service of reception. When the annual commitment service comes, they could renew their baptismal vows individually and, if desired, have hands laid on them. This might unwarrantably be interpreted as initiatory by some of course.

Secondly those already baptized (but with the old services of baptism) and as yet unconfirmed, whether adult or children, could be welcomed regularly to communion without awaiting the annual commitment service. This would show that the latter service was not initiatory, however pastorally desirable, and that initiation was sacramentally complete in baptism.

APPENDIX 2: CHURCH OF ENGLAND VIEWS ON CONFIRMATION AND THE USES OF THE LAYING ON OF HANDS IN THE BIBLE

A main issue to establish about Confirmation is as to what actions constitute it. An item however on which all agree is that it includes as central the laying on of hands, often a bishop's hands, and usually with prayer for defending, enduing, strengthening, confirming or in some way coming of the Holy Spirit. A second feature is the use of oil, or chrism, which is poured on or used to sign the candidate with the cross. The oil can even be made up of more than one ingredient. Thirdly there is the signing of the person with the sign of the cross or consignation, and a fourth feature introduced optionally into the Series 2 baptism service is the giving of a lighted candle. In the Hippolytan initiation rite and others since, there have of course been many other items also. Rome's new suggested Confirmation service interestingly lays more emphasis on the renewal of baptismal vows which has also been part of Anglican services at all stages. However the issue is slightly simplified when the constituting actions are assessed from the New Testament. No one has as yet tried to find more than the laying on of hands and chrism from it, though in the case of the laying on of hands, the hands have been claimed to be those of bishops in succession to or after the example of the apostles, and the gift of the Holy Spirit has been also associated with this laying on of hands. Both these facets are justified primarily on the basis of Acts 8. The same passage together with Acts 19 has been taken as justifying a second quite separate and later stage in initiation by some, while others argue for one initiation rite with two logically and theologically separate parts.

A second issue concerns the theological meaning of this supposed rite. Here the Liturgical Commission's useful introduction to their Series 2 services helpfully lays out three views as current in the Church of England. The first or Reformed or Evangelical view is stated rightly as being that baptism in water is the sacramental means by which the Spirit is given to Christians, confirmation being the occasion when Christians renew the acts of repentance and faith made in their name, or by themselves if adults, at their baptism. This all takes place in the bishop's presence and he prays for and blesses them. God may well meet with the candidates at this time. The second view agrees that baptism in water is the sacramental means by which the Spirit is given to Christians. Confirmation is seen as a second sacramental act later, consisting of prayer for the coming of the Holy Spirit and a laying on of hands. It effects a further work of the Spirit, assisting the candidates to grow in the Christian life and strengthening them against temptation. J. D. C. Fisher describes this view as 'generally held in the mediaeval Western church'. The third view, which Fisher himself holds, and which is commonly known as the Mason-Dix line, believes that baptism in water together with hand-laying constitutes the sacramental means by which Christians receive the Spirit. If the two sacramental acts are distinguished in thought, or separated in practice, the Spirit is believed to come in baptism to effect regeneration and cleansing from sin and in confirmation to complete the divine indwelling.

A third issue concerns the variety of purposes for which hands were laid on in the Bible. Quite often they were laid on the sick Mk. 6.5; 7.32f; 8.23f; Lk. 4.40; 13.13; Acts 9.12,17. They seem here to assure the invalid of the gift of healing. It is of course possible to interpret Acts 8 and 19 thus, the hands assuring the disciples that they have the gift of the Holy Spirit. At other times they are used to assure the person of or to convey to the person a blessing (Gen. 48.14; Mk. 10.16). These could alternatively be interpreted as an extension of the idea of identifying oneself with the person or object, as seems to be the main meaning in Lev. 1.4; 24.14. Setting people apart for a particular spiritual purpose seems the aim in Num 8.10; 27.18-23; Dt. 34.9 and Acts 6.1-6; 13.1-3; 1 Tim. 4.14; 2 Tim. 1.6 (which looks like ordination!). R. E. O. White in *The Biblical Doctrine of Initiation* sums up the underlying meaning as 'the identification of one person with another by touch so as to focus one's will, judgment, guilt or authority upon another.'

APPENDIX 3: ACTS 8 AND 19—SOME FURTHER THOUGHTS

J. D. G. Dunn has aptly called Acts 8.4-24 the riddle of Samaria. He analyses six solutions to the basic problem that the Samaritans are said to believe and are then baptized, but do not receive the Spirit until the apostles' hands are later laid on them.

Of the three most probable solutions to Acts 8, Dunn argues quite persuasively against the idea that what was given through the hands was not the Spirit himself but his dramatic gifts or charismata, the Spirit having himself been given at belief-baptism. He is less persuasive against Lampe's popular view that because Samaria was in a unique position vis-a-vis the Jerusalem church, God withheld his Spirit at their belief-baptism in order to welcome them and reassure both them and the Jerusalem apostles, by giving the Spirit through the welcoming gesture of their hands. His own fresh and fascinating view is to claim that despite belief and baptism they were not yet Christians, and this awaits their full understanding when the apostles came. Then they respond and so receive the Spirit, *the* hall-mark of a Christian. However well he argues, his own view remains open to criticisms. Whatever the true explanation, Acts 8 can hardly support the idea of a second initiatory act of laying on of hands bringing the Spirit, in the light of the evidence on the Spirit and baptism already amassed and the New Testament's silence elsewhere.

Much the same can be said of the Ephesian disciples in Acts 19.1-7. This time the baptism and the laying on of hands are at the same time vv.5,6. Indeed these verses could well be translated: 'they were baptized in the name of the Lord Jesus and, Paul having laid hands on them, the Holy Spirit came on them'. Thus at most we have two parts of one rite.

The true explanation of Acts 19 does not seem far to seek. Only two terms would suggest that the twelve men were already Christians before Paul arrived—*'mathetai'* meaning 'disciples', and *'pisteusantes'* meaning 'having believed' in verses 1 and 2. However about the first term, the significant factor is Luke's omission of the definite article and the addition of 'certain'. When Luke wants to describe all the Christians in an area he invariably uses *'the* disciples' Acts 6.7; 9.19,38. By using 'certain' and no article, he seems to be distinguishing these twelve men from the other Christians at Ephesus. The term 'believed' could then refer to Paul's charitable or even mistaken assumption. However both words point to some connection with Christ, and suggest that they were not merely disciples of John the Baptist, but probably among those many (compare Acts 19.13-16; Mk. 9.38-40; Mt. 7.22) who must have heard and responded to part of Jesus' message, having previously been baptized by John before going home to Ephesus or wherever, without perhaps even knowing about the Cross, Resurrection or Pentecost. Thus they are in a way similar to those very doubtful Christians in Samaria. If therefore Dunn is right on Acts 8, the laying on of hands is twice used as the method to merge people into mainstream Christianity.